CW00705728

Donald McMorran

SONNETS

AUSTIN MACAULEY
PUBLISHERS LTD.

Copyright © Donald McMorran (2016)

The right of Donald McMorran to be identified as author of this work has been asserted by him in accordance with section 77 and 78 of the Copyright, Designs and Patents Act 1988.

All rights reserved. No part of this publication may be reproduced, stored in a retrieval system, or transmitted in any form or by any means, electronic, mechanical, photocopying, recording, or otherwise, without the prior permission of the publishers.

Any person who commits any unauthorized act in relation to this publication may be liable to criminal prosecution and civil claims for damages.

A CIP catalogue record for this title is available from the British Library.

ISBN 978 1 84963 960 6 (Paperback)
ISBN 978 1 84963 961 3 (E-Book)

www.austinmacauley.com

First Published (2016)
Austin Macauley Publishers Ltd.
25 Canada Square
Canary Wharf
London
E14 5LB

SONNETS 1

One time lucky soon, one time soon, one time that I may win, for me to win, to win, to win the bell chimes in.

In huddling puddle, a puddle of the rubble.

The rubble that I do not own for me. For me for me to have as my own things, things that are mine, mine I say, mine, mine to have.

Forever more, and that was that for that was that.

For mine, yes mine is often afraid of things forgotten.

Forgotten in a day time day.

Of day, of day, of day and night time soon, for soon enough was day. And soon it was a silver morning in the window, noon, noonday, noontime, noon.

For noon was noon, and night was night, and day came again soon. In nowhere, unbelievable in nevertheless.

SONNETS 2

In nevertheless land, win O, wind O, win am I a win O, please
some past me again for thee a wind for my sails of due, and
soon enough the blue time o flight, the blue bird flies enough
for me. Enough, enough, for me for me enough, enough for
me.
For it became a wool wear for me song.
And once upon the merry river, the merry river, ran to me. For
I was a merry way the tide be tidy, tidy, tides.
For I'll a love a good may song and rite.
For please forgive you me.

And I desire that it will always be a special time, for our
rhyme in song, song that I never forget, forget me nots, in
snowdrops, falsely, falsetto you me. Falsely falsetto you me
you me falsely falsetto you me.

SONNETS 3

Water and oil
Carob and tea
A touch of
Varnish.

Please remember
Watercolours.
Though shopping I
Write.

Distant distances for
Paintings to go
Lost in the
Diffusing wheel.

Maybe year I'll count a few pictures too gone away. For a
fish mildly wins. A line draws the line in embroiderer's
excitement. What an interesting train. A marvellous railway
for a book of time.

SONNETS 4

One fine time I wandered merrily nowhere through invention of landscape. A funny old, old weathery mews. Happy finds for mannequin.

One day you'll discovery you, one day because I am a writing, a writing, a drawing for a singing time.

For time never near and seamster's knittings for cravats tiny statues made of thread. A painting by wool and leafy colour in time for another day the same day, through pencil.

And I received you gained wind in the plains.

I believed in stratagem. You believed in dreams old some photographical easy to find. Easy to give and to find forever again. I knew paint and paper.

I know that Art is worthwhile because of knitting wool.

Art
That is therapy to me
Such
A time as for
Art
Only invented
Yet true to paper
New and in photography
From tree to still life
And figurative from colour of a seamster's values.

Thanks I say thanks to me did you hear me say thanks to me.

The time beyond, beyond the whiles for me. I believe in may song, song, no sing along for time will come for peace, and while, and while for me. For it seems to you for me and for me. I never know you a thing for thee too a thing, a thing, a thing, a ling a tie to sing.

And one time less
And less
And more
And one
Time
Because because
Of thaw in the wintertime of less of less
And less
Of forever
In the winter day
At that little summery
Tea time time that
Time that
Time you best
Remember
Yet you remember
That time that time best forgot
Or forgotten
That time of goodbye
That special
Time of you forgot
That time of time
Be forgot.
Time time of time
Be forgot
And one time seen
It seems that
I was one day soon a tree
For a day.

And one day soon enough, the time was arising, arising, arising, arising, yet for me, for I may go, for I may go, a loitering, a loitering, a loitering a wondering, a wondering, after my art this time, of time, this time. For when it few, it few.

SONNETS 5

For me oils and pattern to you. Watercolours oily pages. Fun pottery for glazes in water for watercolour paper. Paper, paper for painting. Painting of invention. Landscape and vernacular, words and portraits. What a rumple dumpling. TV for a brush and a spoon.

For me so becoming a time to give Art so too had I Art to give. It seemed nice that Art might be forthcoming and forevermore kind of steaming along and fashionable. In poetry there was a time or a mixture for rhyme like a special cascade knitting and a picture.

SONNETS 6

There'll be a fun saying there'll be a fun saying in life. And that saying that old, old saying that saying splendid, splendid for me for me for this much thanks.

I remember that thou art a handwritten man because thou art a man of many, many dreams for thee, for thee many dreams for thee, truly and by thee. For thee for thee, on ornamental shadow for thee. Yet beyond into the last pages.

And paint
Was
Water
To me
To use.

Was it never time soon. Art yes, Art was what time for spring a little statuette. For this and thanks around. By a train.

To mine splendid day. A happy Art in passing time. A watercolour of founded font is special to give away. For thou art needy of Art.

And from hereon and thereafter I should say a lovely parcel and a fine Art to see and send space to you of Art.

Such fun in a time of saying some prose of saying.

Wool.O
Wool
That I might
Have just
A darn not more for me to keep
Despite modern values.

To me, to me, me not a single please. Please not please. Please O please for this time for what it's worth I believe in time spent receiving for me I mean not what I say to me true by by by by blarney O sing of me to me to receive to me.

Saying that there there and for me. Me not thee thee I say thee.

Thee for me for this I have, I have a time in mind mindfully.

I see you
And I see you yes
You this fine sunny day
Because
I am a fellow
Man a fellow man
I am because of this of this today
I shall be a fellow man
And one day
I shall be a man a man a
Man a music man
And for a time.

And one day
Soon you'll
Be a special
One to me to me
A special one
To me.

And one day soon it seems that I was one day soon a free for a day. And one day soon a free away, away, away, a day, away, away, away.

SONNET 7

Once in time
I became
A
Story for this much
Thanks so was
I
A story so story
Was I a
Someone.

Someone endeavouring in all the same for life was a picture, a perfect picture. An endeavour that might seem something, something in time. For in the beginning trumpets sound and trumpets soft softly never to be forgot. In a playful picture it seemed to be the marvellous time of seeing time go by. In tonality half a dozen rhymes, rhymes a dozen, a dozen songs. Songs so fleeting songs so full of sadness.

SONNETS 1

Please forgive me for I am an artist, I am, I am an artist. It is so sad. I am a painter of landscapes imagined. Forgive you me.

For it
Seemed
Life was
Trade
Yet life was made.
Yes life

Was made,
Made for a merchant's life.
What it be made
Made for what.

Made
Say I say that
I made Art.
Yes Art by me.
Yes Art by me
And philatelic
Philatelic.

I know that I ought to trade
For Art Art
From me.

Art that was worth
And more, more trains.

Forgotten times in days. For I am a scoundrel of art called a minstrel so minstrel me O my for a time to fry food food. Food food that not yes in that platter for a poetical time of store. Now store so time for poetry and storage. Such food so few few the colours for a painting of pottery few few can decide the left of times forgotten. Learning for a picture that I bequest into times of long jesting jesting for a painting. And a timeful time of times that not a fish.

You'll never do a word. A thing a rhyme a time for me. A time always always for a poem and always for a time to remember remember remember that I am a person of in exactitude of manners and of character. Character so upset that believe that that was a time of successful writing. Of a time so far far away. That I'm a fool for the times of landscapes and of rose's sunsets of incredible stature. Of a time when for my time my time. I am yes I am involved or betide time. That means that I am a good person of art by art. Forgotten are my times for art.

One day I loved too much and served too little. A time when I ate and had stars in mine eyes. No music for me. Yet may the food that music be let that be and be played and please give me so much that I owe and. Yet let it be forever glorious. And I say yet in terms of somewhat perilous a way. Please let me play that I may play and for a special day. A day so rare. So rare that I may and never shall ever be a wonder likely thee.

I know that I ought to trade
For Art Art
From me.

For it
Seemed
Life was
Trade
Yet life was made.
Yes life.

And
I
Received you gained wind
In the Plaines.

17

I believed in stratagem
You believed in dreams
Old some photography
Easy to find.
Easy
To give, and to find forever again.
I
Knew paint
And
Paper.

SONNETS 2

The time beyond the whiles for me I believe in may song song no sing along for me will come for peace and while and while for me. For it seems to you for me and for me. I never know you a thing for thee too a ting a thing a thing a ling a time to sing.

I see you
And I see you yes
You this fine sunny day
Because
I am a fellow
Man a fellow man
And one day I shall be a man a man a
Man a music man
And for a time

And one time less
And less
And more
And one
Time
Because because
Of thaw in the wintertime of less of less
And less
Of forever
In the winter day
That little summery
Tea time time that
Time tat
Time you best
Remember
Yet you remember
That time that time best forgot
Of forgotten
That time of goodbye

That special
Time of you forgot
That time of time
Be forgot
Time time of time
Be forgot
And one time soon
It seems that
I was one day soon a free
For a day.
And one day
Soon you'll
Be a special
One to me to me
A special one
To me.

And one day soon enough the time was arising arising arising arising yet for me for I may go for I may go a loitering a loitering a wondering a wondering after my art this time of time this time. For when it few it few.

And one day soon it seems that I was one day soon a free for a day. And one day soon a free away away away a day away away away.

SONNETS 1

Time time
And time
Enough
For me me
Me.
Maybe except me I'll come
To Thee
Again.

And it was
A time of values
Woe begotten
A time of gotten
Down low and still woe begotten
I remember.

Nothing except specially steam
Pillars left.
Left and departed.
Even lews mews tough shoes.
A little apprehension.
Yes it was pleasant thought vet.
What dost one know
Never to find.

I remember too. You're for music mine. Say it were true for you and me mine day was fun and it was very pouring with pain. Lo behold the rain will come again today I'll be a new bird bird birds to me my dear dearest one at making out a playful rhyme. A rhyme a rhyme for me. For me and for this this time of day.

SONNETS 2

One
Fine day for Art.
One fine day,
One
Fine day.
It's one those days.

Woe betide Those days of Art.
The special days
Of fine that
Thou
Art made
In exact exacting
Exactitude
And for pity's time in
Form and triumph
Doth that falls from upon
High
Visit
Like a bird and tumbles and errs yet never
Banks for me
It was true yet it may
Be.

To be understood that thou art bold when
Thou hast much opinion
Opinions opinions
Dear dearest misgotten

Betide thy times of fishes.
Yet still not by what one can never
Count yet still.

NOVEL 1

I like to write to iotas of my own. Not of my own possession but of one iota drawn in bird. A bird in flight to a drawing, that might one day be a painting.

You never knows it but I know a Poet that's an Artist. Called an Artist by say called an Artisan. And one day you'll soon discovery me a lyrical story yet I Art History. Now when I sing I sing not a note not a beaut but a picture. Please sitter tattle tattle down the wind. I say it was a picture ain't it true. Because of course you know me and I don't know you the picture. One cay you may soon see a picture that'll be the time of a mixture.

I remember you that you were a one person in it all former yes that's a me say me and one day it came to pass me by what I will discovery thee a lyrical thee and a history of me. Now when I sing along chick a chock cheep I believe in thee please whistle down the window win a lot window whistle down the window ain't it true because you believe in that old song repetition after me that's for me not for thee.

You became soon I became told that's an old old Artist and Artist I am told. Someday soon say I away say and I'll be away into Natural History or please say I a picture.

Please give me a juniper juniper June July July for an artist an artist in bloom. For soon it seeming of lyrical waxing waxing for thee. A piece of wax it waxing for thee. Thee times of yours forsooth it weren't a time or a timing for say I say Jove. For it seeming to me an incredible, And by the by it seeming to me an incredible time of not and forgot forget-me-nots. Forget-me-nots for time in time away. For soon it may be June again time again. Humpty hop for furrowing and tarring and fiddle dee flop.

Certain ye be and certain ye be to me and to thee certain certain ye be for a real real time. For in time after rhyme you'll be the fortune and I'll be the misery misery for thee please please sing for me. Me and me a gelatine for me. And by the by in time try I try to build I try to build an art house song cheerio hooray hooray was good but cheerio was better better some fine day. Of winter sold in June.

For me not for thee. Don't know it a song. Don't know it a song and don't know it a song for me and not for thee. For thee and not for a note for a song not a timing temporal and rhyming please fiddle dee dee for a violoncello will come to thee that's for certain certain ye be.

SONNETS 9

There's something brilliant there's something brilliant as far
as I can
See called being an Englishman an Englishman
A very very very Englishman.
And someday be might go away go away
A very very very very Englishman.
And soon enough time became time
Became time again.
Time again to write.
And soon again to sing again to sing a song be sung
To sung to sing a song be sung.
And there will be time again to write and write and write.
And one day the time became over the time became over the
time the time became over for tea and tarmacadam.
And then there was a time when time
Was waltz with honey that time
That sweet day sweet sweet
Time of day.
Why that old honey a time
A time and never rhyme
And time and never rhyme
In time forever a honey chime.

How way dolly how way duly how way dolly lie lie dear boy
how dolly lie lie.
Perchance in time time time
Time time perchance
In time time time.

And one summer's day one summer's day
Only own alone
And own and alone

Shall make me tick and tock
Shall make tick and tock and tock.
And by the by it came to see why honey.
And me was honey and me and why it came to pass
That the honey you have is the honey you have.
So buy the time see for me a merchant's song.
And buy and buy and buy the time again home again
Quick. That old engine that motor it motored on slow and
never
Before did it travel again.

And they come
And they come come come
And they come they come for poetry
They come
Come come
They come again for poetry
They come again for poetry.
And for soon it may come come
For poetry for poetry
For poetry for cake and coffee
For love and honey
For love of all that
All that jazz.

And soon enough you'll dry your dishes
And make a wish.
For sign in time
Some time has come to pass
It became it became known
Known to a single little bird
That old who are many shall never one
Shall never be one shall never be one.
And by and I soon deny that I have a joy a joy a joy in store

A store that is seldom strong
And the time sooner you'll soon deny
That you are a tyrant a despicable and a Biro over the hills to
Dover to Dover say.

Piece O cake
And pieces of eight.
Perchance for psalm perchance
For bread perchance
For margarine.
Remember fire boil and cauldron bubble
Fire burn cakes ye burn and cauldron bubble
Fires turn and fires burn
Fires turn and fires burn.
Perchance a day perchance
A way for me my song and sing.
Dear boy dear boy thou art a boy dear boy
Dear boy thou
Art for forgive thee forgive forgive forgive thee forgive.

Flutter-by sows flutter-by the woodpecker woodpecker rose
flutter away and by the time the time the time dear
Time for time and away may change the tides of mine.
Fair thee well said I pip pip cheerio cheerio away cheerio.
For once in time in time dear
Soon for once in once dear
Time. Lost forever and a day
Lost forever and a day lost forever
And a way away.
Forever forever someday
Forever time for tea time
For terrible terrible tea.

SONNETS 5

And now and now and now you're a man of the pen that's a
man to tell the tale the
Tale of a time forever a time in tune the time the time in tune.

For each rhyme began boring boring boring.

For one time more or one time less there came to be
something see something to see something to see.

SONNETS 6

It seems that you were a one a one unknown to me in all in all forever and a day to pass me by my side of things now and then a tie for sat sum parallels in the dawn of time of time for me and for my song.

I remember mine time for mine rhyme and mine dress and all in all it was unfair unfair it was it was unfair. Because by thee when I chisel to me I will know yes I'll know what will bring will bring to ballad a ballad of a balladeer mine true true time of year. For a year in time of my old time time tambourine. And one day a harmonica didn't come my way because of course I do I do do for sing a sing song for me. For me for sing along sing for thee.

Why it's a song I don't know it at all for it was a fay and a fay sor a play for a say sung sung see note see for thee this paradigm for e a sing along timing and rhyming alive.

SONNETS 7

For a while a while a while a whiles in the whiles.
Tweedledee. For I believe in maybe something something.
For me for me truly truly. For me me I mean me me lyrical me
me bring me bring ling ling for thee the cheer cheep cheerio. I
friend thee not to say for me and not for thee for thee.

And now I come come time time time for time is what I come
for for it means it means a peace for time.
As time doesn't go doesn't go for time for for
For me for then and their shells so joyful for a wasp and a sea.

A wasp and a time a time for a time for a time and neither a
robe or a dress for a pastime pass time in fashion for thee.

SONNETS 4

And play son
Play
Son stay
That you're
A man of our
Times
That's a man of time begone
To tell the tale
To sing the time go by go by to sing the time a way a way to
sing the time in time away to sing the time in time.

Forever more forever archery bore O bore forever
since time began began began began began. And soon a time
will come to pass for time passes passes by.

For time
Passes
In its own time
In passing
Time time flies like a bird in song.
For time time a time O time since time was.

Since time was what I was was on writing me dear
me for I am scoffed what I am scoffed and cloth and thee sear
meal for thee one day you'll give me something for a cheese a
cheese by cheese by cheese.

And by the time I am on song shine a fellow rhyme.
Rhyme rhyme a fellow rhyme I have no time my cloth dear
man misses thy man fa-loo foray fa-loo today a fellow misses
thine cloth for one such noon you'll be a fool a fool for me
and for thee a juniper for weensy come weensy go.

For the time it came round again prepare yourself that
thou art a little fool for thee.

Thy troth for mimes you and me far far away far far betide thine time of where far away bethought betimes of tides betide begone where time slides away remember thee one sunny sunny day for me.

By morns day next next next Sunday next I'll remember thee that day of roses roses roses for mine work for mine that thee may have. For soon you'll see for soon you'll see sighing come to thee. For in the day of thine and more time and me.

Because because of sawing and seeing of fleeting dust in the canopy. For if there ever was a time of sawing and seeing then it was a time for me.

By this or by that by that or by little little old sunshine tea. You remember that funny sunny day. By the way side say that I am a good berry go root rot in the way the way of time and tea.

For sighing searing weary tides the tide where best forgotten left untold mine own grave mistake mistaken me the same. For in the scraps the scraps of daytime of daytime tides of left of line and line be told the disappearance of a colour forsooth it sounds be sounds be sounds the time the time of waiting sublime. For in sublimit betide sublimit endlessly a brilliance be thought it it were not me.

And by the way of it the way of it the way of it I was best got unrest until I rested free free for an hour an hour to write to write again per se per se thee not thee not for see nor see to go.

SONNETS 3

By mine troth how stuffed I am on writing dear fellow. I am so stuffed that I have no troth. My cloth dear fellow misses thee. One day soon you'll discovery me what not sit for thee and for thee a juniper June berry. For cheese come cheese go fa la la to thee.

And by the time it came back again I soon misunderstood that you that thou art a bounding bacon of a man so bounding thou art that thou must never cry little red duckling again for thou and for me.

Forsooth dear sunny mimes mimes you me. For far begone my tides of time where bygones be bygones where time slips away. I remember thee one fine served Sunday you me.

And one day you'll discover that you're a good man and a good man you'll be a good man and a good man you'll be a good an a good man you'll be a bygone be bygone a bygone you'll be.

Strong tea dear soul strong tea.
Strum away soul
Strum on.
My life away in time a take time away.

And by the by
I am forever
In sincerity
Mine forever lavender groves.

And one day soon
You'll discover that thou art
A man O time
And timing sincerity
SINCERITAS FELICITAS
And be gone neither

Me nor yes yes
Small see for thou art
A maiden voyage in time
Forgot ten fecklessly forgotten ye me ye'll be sincerity for
thee.

Now when again home again country swan song
stand and swan down swan down again soon by lingo sing
along song sang she the best on times wells and begone wells
time lest forgot best forgotten.

And soon a song
A song away
Tune gone
Gone away tune lest
Forget it's gone
Gone away tune lest forgot best forgotten.

And soon a song a
Song a song
Away tune gone gone
Away tune
Lest forgot its gone gone in March and May time time to stay.

I remember you that you were a one person in it all
forever yes that a me me I say me and one day it came to pass
me by that I will discovery thee a lyrical thee and a history of
me.

Now when I sing along chick a cha-ck cha-ck cheep
the window win a lot window whistle down the window ain't
it true because you believe in that old song repetition after me
that's for me not for thee.

For me not for thee. Don't I know it a song. Don't I
know it a song and don't I know of a song for me and not for

thee. For thee and not for a note for a song not a timing tempo and rhyming please fiddle dee dee for a violoncello will come to thee that's for certain certain ye be for a real real time,

For in time after rhyme you'll be the fortune and I'll be the misery misery me so sing a song not a song not a song for thee please please sing for me.

Me and me
A gelatine for me.

And by the by in time
Try
I try
To build hooray
Hooray
Was good
But cheerio was better
Better some fine day
Of winder sold
In June.

SONNETS 3

To mine splendid day. A happy Art in passing time. A watercolour of founded font is special to give away. For thou art needy of Art.

Art
That is therapy to me.
Such
A time as for
Art
Only invented
Yet true to paper
New and in photography
From tree to still life
And figurative from colour of a seamster's values.

SONNETS 2

You never know it come on its great to live.
For
A time of my own and a tome.
For
Something and forever never
In never never write
And in never ever write land
And one day soon enough
There came a chime
For me.
Which was a lily
A lily of the lilies.
By the by tide by
Contrite bye bye bye.

SONNETS 11

Flutter-by sows flutter-by the woodpecker woodpecker rose
flutter away and by the time the time
The time dear time for time and away may change the tides of
mine.
Fair thee well said I pip pip cheerio cheerio away cheerio.
For once in time in time dear
Soon for once in once dear
Time. Lost forever and a day
Lost forever and a day lost forever
And a way away.
Forever forever someday
Forever time for tea time
For terrible terrible tea.

SONNETS 5

It became a time
A long way off
Where I will blow my horn again
Home again home
Counting the tiles
Again pottery beat.
For sing sang
She sang sing sang song
You'll soon discovery me
You'll soon sing to my tourney tune.
Sing along fandango
Fandango you me. One day
You'll feel like it writing again.
Writing can be such fun
All over a silver point
World
Where there can be
Where there can be
Flowers a-bloom engines too for a few
More time ago,
Times ago soon magic time.
Soon again once again write again
Beat please read again
Write again write again beat yes write.
Yes chip
Chip sit chip
Chip wood chip choppy.
Carry on calamity train
Calamity carries on calamity train. One day
You'll know to write it to write it in
Spontaneity to write it to me.
And soon enough
It became known that life
Is a sad one perchance
You a gone home a sad one

One life. By the way by the way good
Art say. A cheerful
So say O.

SONNETS

And then one day the writing wasn't good enough so I
decided to write with dough and suet
Dough and suet that's what I say.
And one day it came to pass
It came to pass
And then one day it didn't happen again.
The sale of the bread.
Because of course the meanings
Of a cup of tea.
For the sake of a pass
At tea and two slices.

It's about you you you the artist. It's about red yellow and
blue.
It's about tree big small and horn by Weathering colours.
You know what the mean genie eye gene Jean.
Come on there fellow, genie eyed gene.
What else what else but a vase and waltz, a waltz for me.

You never close your eyes without goodbye
You never close your eyes without some sigh
You never close your eyes without a try for the spring come
when it may.
That song bird will fly fly away
Yes it'll fly fly fly away
'till the blue birds come
and they come we'll smile
For it's a while to smile.
For you never know it 'till a song bird's sung and then flown.

And it came to past me a fish and a sea. It came past me a fish
and a sea.

And a drivel drove by and a drivel drove by and he dove bye
bye.

41

And it came past me a fish and a sea. It came past me a fish
and a sea.

You'll never know it a Juno in July a Juno in July you'll take
it a Juno in July
Yes some might say it vain like weather vane in spun a
weather vane in spun some might say it
And know it enjoy time of the poet.

And after all that all that brash music there cometh a time
when I shall play a drum.
The living drum the drum knower the rhymes of the pen and
the tell, the lines and the sublimes the signs of the times.

Don't you never do it don't you ever do I'm a diamond you're
a gem you're a fantastic little stone
Don't you ever do it climb and jump and run and all.
And then one day when I came to play to catch a trick in the
long long corn. And then I ate lemon and ham.

As the sea smashed the beach the yin yang sang and the
butterflies rose.
Told you so said the woodpecker told you so said the
woodpecker again. For the stonemason
Chipped and chipped away.
Palatable to say more palatable and won't say more.

And before it was too late for tour o move on to kingdom
come. At last another line to descend upon.

With this and that drivel and all. And then suddenly a bird
flew by and I became a bird painter.
Wowed and the bird flew by vowed path e. path e I can see in
every sing.

You never close your eyes

Without a goodbye you never close your eyes without some
sigh you never close your eyes without a try for the Spring.
Come when it may.
That song bird will fly fly away 'till the blue birds come and
they come and they come we'll smile for it's a while to smile.
For you never know it 'till a song bird's sung and then flown.
And a drivel drove by and a drivel drove by and he dove bye
bye.
And it came past me a fish and a sea. It came past me a fish
and a sea.
You'll never know it a Juno in July a Juno in July you'll take
it a Juno in July yes some might say it vain like a weather
Vain in spun weather vane in spun some might say it and
know it enjoy time of the poet.
And after all that all that brash music there cometh a time
when I shall play a drum. The living drum the drum
Knower the thymes of the pen and the tell, the lines and the
sublimes the signs of the times.
Don't you never do it
Don't you ever do I'm a diamond you're a gem you're a
fantastic little stone don't you ever do it climb and jump and
Run and all. And then one day when I came to play to catch a
trick in the long long corn. And then I ate lemon and
Ham. Sometimes it's clear I'm clear in a kind of a way.
I'm as clear as can make it a second a do and fin it and wink it
and sink it again. It went for cheer and it went near
And for cheer what a wonderful present to receive on Noel to
receive again,
'T was the night before Noel and the fling flung me a bell ring
rung me a bell sing sung me a bell that I would never ski past
and never before. Your handwriting is to lyrical and logical
too lyrical and logical get real you know what
Yes you know what a thing. And that's the end of it all fungal
and fungals and Tweedledee and Tweedledee.
So this wheel
It spinner much and it spinner slow puff puff puff.
And then one day as it came along mesmeric and magically it
came a time the writing went away

In a spin and a short
And a day, forever and a way.
Summer and winter and summer in May
The top of the fill the time wrong the time soon gone. A turn
bye bye and a turn so long. A turn ho for the seasons so.
And that's what it does it does a jig in the May time.

A bulb and a tea. And that was it for the baker her were.
Maybe of course
There was a train a train in November, a sweet old train. And
in that train there was a sort of life a life of a man
Who needed no understanding
And no understanding. For his samba his way and his cheer.

And the waltz Walt and the waltz Walt and the waltz take z
waltz and the z waltz z tango. And for z chime take z chime.
By the by huh.

You're not those people over there
You know those people there
They're not you at all they're not you you know mister man
so build it and build away home.
Sometime soon you see the windswept come from wedge
wood way the canal barges go and stop. But one day
Man can build a home and by the by he can build one in a
year.
Soon summers here.

And then one day a squirrel came along and ate an apple on a
branch and then one day the squirrel want away and
Was gone. And then one day at the end of a route
Of a pen I decided upon my pen.
Put down the pen door open the paper make us some writing
writing for paper faster than ham and faster than lime
To make us through the wood.
Faster through the wood faster. It is never done
So stop a pen.

Nor a wheel nor a sprig.
Hooray for a pen.

Once upon a rhyme dear rhyme
Please tell me a time that all the things I have never heard
please tell me here again again please tell me here
Again. Hum go
The bees the apple at its knees
Falling from the tree again
For the bee to eat.
Bees bees buzzy bees bees to eat the apple ho
Forever to eat the apple ho.

And still the day.
She went away and joyful was her name until
One time she found a climb of pink and lilac blue and one day
it became her due.
Surely sometimes there's times
For flowers surely sometimes there's hours of flowers.
To speak the story to speak and play.
And do the writing
Player the man
With the emerald at the end of the day.

Stop frowning
What happened to the remains of the days' time?
Without sadness said what happened today being a frown. Just
for the love of wear and tear and a gown
For I
And for you
The ne'er do well. Sometime in June I'll soon offer a tune
There's a hearth
In a room sometime in June I'll soon offer a tune
There's a hearth
In a room sometime in June I'll offer thee o turn
Again now it's Fall in
Winter again.

But someday of the week
It cometh in time that runners in Marsh ain't playing a tune.
Walking by brick
By nimble and wick
Some say a good wick
Might do me some good.
Some good and a put
Might do me some good and after
That put I'll be a good man
Shall be a good man.
Cook me a dish and I'll eat
A sure fish fishes my me
Some fishes my me me
'O me my me
Some fishes for me.

And by the by
Buy a fish for me for me tea total alone.
Fish fishy for me and fish fishy for thee.
Yes and one day yes, the bell went yes yippee.
You'll never know it but the silent writer is a good writer
Is a good writer
A good writer forever.

Time forgot time
Soon enough the time has flown
Flown away flown away be gone home.
Bygones be beginnings
And beginnings forever lost.
And then one day it became a thing to leave

Beyond the pale of water. It was to leave the anger for a time
of peace
And quiet
And that's life
Life that's gone gone away.
And then of course
It became simple
Simple poem
Simple simple little man
Do you know who you are in your own way
Or give and tell
And take and need
And give away forever gone
In time when time forgot
When forgotten was you.
Folly folly folly in praise
Of folly poor me oh my
Give away a time away
In time forgotten me.
Soon betide the time soon gone time in memory time forgot
Soon time began began forgot.

How way dolly how way duly how way dolly lie lie dear boy
how dolly lie lie.
Perchance in time time time
Time time perchance
In time time time,

There's something brilliant there's something brilliant as far
as I can
See called being an Englishman an Englishman
A very very very very Englishman.
And someday be might do away go away
A very very very Englishman.
And soon enough time became time

Became time again
Time again to write.
And soon enough time became time
Became time again.
Time again to write.
And soon again to sing again to sing a song be sung
To sung to sing a song be sung.
And there will be time again to write and write and write.
And one day the time became over the time became over the
time the time became over for tea and
Tarmacadam.
And then there was a time when time
Was waltz with honey that time
That sweet day sweet sweet
Time of day.
Why that old honey a time
A time and never rhyme
And time and never rhyme
In time forever a honey chime.

ART POETRY

The jocund walked and walked and forever walked.
And the jocund had a good life
For the jocund walked. Hey Minnie Mo the moocher the art
writer.
The wishing well the fishing bear
By the wishing well art for art's sake tuppence a time.
And then one day
He came along day came along day came along day to do a
painting
Of a scene of away that was a day worthwhile. You'll never
know it a picture that's there
You'll never know it a picture or believe in what I say a
picture that's there Sometimes on Sundays
There's a picture to see thankfully sometime on sometimes
there's a picture to see.
Don't come the Spring for another snow
In a canvas frame in architecture or in a picture.
Hey bonny no by the banks of the sea over the hills to dry
Over the hills to dry in rag time.

You'll never know it a magic time sorry forget it and knows it
forget it its writing again, writing
Again.
One sonnet afternoon sweet sonnet, afternoon please may I
please give it away my sonnet
Afternoon, and one day I'll be in magic time, forever rhyme
me a rhyme to be a magic time.

Maybe of course
There was a train a train.
And in that train there was a sort of life
A life of a man who needed no understanding
And no understanding.
For his samba his way and his cheer.

And the waltz Walt and the waltz Walt and the waltz take z
waltz and for z waltz z tango.
And for z chime take z chime.
By the by huh you're not those people over there
You know those people there
They're not you you know mister man
So build it and build away home.
Sometime soon you see the winds 'll come from wedge-wood
way
The canal barges go and stop.
But one day man can build a home
And by the by he can build one
In a year. Soon summer's here.
And then one day a squirrel
Came along and ate an apple on a branch
And then one day the squirrel went away
And was gone.
And then one day at the end of a route of a pen
I decided upon my pen.
Put down the pen door open the paper
Make us some writing writing for paper
Faster than ham and faster than time
To make us through the wood.
Faster through the wood faster.
It is never done to stop a pen
Nor a wheel nor a sprig. Hooray for a pen.
Once upon a thyme dear rhyme
Please tell me a time that all the things I have
Never heart please tell me here again
Again please tell me here again.
Hum go the bees the apple at its knees
Falling from the tree again
For the bee to eat.
Bees bees buzzy bees bees to eat the apple ho, forever to eat
the apple ho.
And still the day
She went away and joyful was her name
Until one time she found a climb

Of pink and lilac blue
And one day it became her due.
Surely sometimes there's times for flowers
Surely sometimes there's hours of flowers.
To speak the story to speak and play.
And do the writing player the man with the emerald at the end
of the day.
Stop frowning what happened to the remains
Of the days' time without sadness
Said what happened today
Being a frown.
Just for the love of wear and tear and a gown
For I and for you the ne'er do well.
Sometime in June I'll soon offer a tune
There's a hearth in a room sometime in June.
I'll offer thee no tune again now
It's Fall in winter again.
But someday of the week
It cometh in time that runners in Marsh
Ain't playing a tune.
Walking by brick by nimble and wick
Some say a good wick might do me some good.
Some good and a put might do me some good
And after that put I'll be a good man, shall be a good man.
Cook me a dish and I'll eat a sure fish
Fishes my me some fishes my me me 'O me my me. Some
fishes for me. And by the by buy a fish for
Me for me tea total alone.
Fish fishy for me and fish fishy for thee.
Yes and one day yes, the bell went yes yippee.
You'll never know it but the silent writer
Is a good writer is a good writer
A good writer forever.

Put down the pan
Make us some ham
Put down the pan

Like a butcher makes us some ham it is needed to make us a
wood make us a wood like Mac duff
Make us a wood. It is a wrongful thing to say to have and
have or not to have a wheel. Not to have
A wheel forever not to have.

In a land on an island for far away there was a tree
Again and a train a lovely old main road.
there were plenty there
In that island plenty
Of who needed
No understanding. For his and his cheer for that way
And picture way for picture way and that way.
And for see and song and chime and all.
For see a pick picture pick picture for all they're not of me
they're of you they're of me and me too.
Yes I wish to know it what a picture is worth what a picture is
worth extraordinary though it seems
A picture is worth.
Fortunately that I'm waiting for a train arriving soon.
So lucky to wait not for a cup of tea but for a time
To wait a moment soon.
For some time soon is summer's day the wintry season will
come at stay.
Noon noon day noon and the dong O' the train
A great rush by the by
And then came a chime and the dong went away
All the way all the way.
And because of O' this there was a fine day.
And then one day a squirrel came along
And ate an apple on a branch
And then one day
The squirrel went away and was gone.

And then one day she went away
Another same
Was lady fate. Yes fate was her name
Fate was her name.

And then fortunately enough fate went away, forever fate.
Pink apple and blue went pink apple and blue
So which one's which said I.
Pink apple and red, pink apple and red say I
Pink apple and red.
So long so long fair story
So long say I.
And then one day it went away
But I wanted the saying for,
Two cans to mustard due.
And the writing, quoth the man with epicure
At the hairdressers in the noon day.
Stop clowning what happened to something sad
Without sadness and what happened say you
To someone being a clown
Just for the frill of it
Wearing a gown
Say I and the ne'er do well.
Sometime in soon
I'll offer thee a rhyme. In soon
In time I'll offer thee no rhymes again.
Don't cry for me
Because I love skiing
Summer time and summer time and sometime like always
I like ski sing song down a tide O' snow.
Snow on the low bank.
Celebrations, celebrations,
Celebrations
For summer's here.

A SONG O' WATER

And then one day I went along strum a strum strum with my
harp a task to do yet a task to do and
Then one day the task went away.
And then one day I decided upon to sing a song
For feign or come rhyme.
That'll be the day
When I sing my song.
My song O' tuna
For a can O' salt water.
Forever the salt for a plaster O' paint.
We'll meet up again forever and a day.
Yes forever and a day. That's just
And that's what they say said Justine,
That's what they say
Sayer O'mine
That little old yarn.
This is the way that they go away
To two by two.
All along all along me
To buy a fresh pen
To think a little picture
A picture for me.
With its rights and its wrongs its best
And its songs.
Its timings claimable
Hey ho.
I soon discovered that I hadn't a clue
And by the by a baker's interest
Is he hadn't a cupboard.
Ex ho-mines librettist
A baker's bop and a loaf
And by the by a bulb and a tea.
And that was it for the baker he were.

SONNETS 4

You never know
It but I believe in miracles of moulding, mouldings decorative.

Twenty a pace twenty a pace
A horse's race.

For Rudolph the artist
Is here come cheerio the time
With a red painted nose.

Once upon a time Robins
And daffodils say the sparrows and the bells
Of Clements ringing.
And one special day I went and ran
Away to song.
You'll never know it the song I never know
go the birds and so
Do their feet,
You'll never know
What my season is
Except in June
For I always say by Jove.
Fortune
And I fortune
And I and a black pen.
Butterfly's rose,
Mould you so
Said the woodpecker
Chipped
And chipped away.
A for a rose C or a squirrel D for a woodpecker
And all run away.
By the wayside bye the wayside little Robin.
I've changed. Woe betide the tide the time for something

O' some one
To behold that I have
Fame and frames besides the sprigs and cogs
Of that fair time O'trading
Tray ding-a-ling-a-ling-my old man.
Fling sometime sometime sometime that old man fining fin-
gee sum sum.
By the way
Fumblings how came it thou
It came to me to tell thee how
To might write
And be fortunate to
Milk a cow how now brown cow how now.
Sometime again you'll know me now
That I'm no feline foe
And then again I seem to be
A bit of a fool.
Thou art a fool
My dear my dear old pal for thou art better than a day
By the way it seems to me to you
To you you look like good old.
And one time more and one time less.
I've been to see the way.
And by the by O' by the by goodbye. For farewell.
Tweedledee for a long way off I'll say to thee to me me me.
I'll say to me.
For time in time you'll see
That time again I'm free.
Free O' trouble free O' woe
Sometime a bee hive seen a long way off.
Math blown my feathered top knot off.
Away away the winds and the rains
You'll come again to beside the rain
The rain fandango. Fandango ye me
O' we to move and run away.
O' we to move and run to stray
Run non-nee run.
For come it time a time splendid a time in thou art mercy me.

Doesn't seem to be
Caught again for thee prithee pardon
Pardon a nut.
Pardon a nut down town. Right about around
We go around around around. A round a time in space.
Me cod a cod of orange in splendour in splendour be.
Astride a fair
Fair carousel to sell before
And then it was a picture
Of to me time again.
For in the carousel there was a horse of splendours wonder.
And one tie one time
More for are yes art one time
Iota one time
Fun-dinging ionic funder of time.
That time that time more less of mine.
And then one day time time it came to me
To write some rhyme some rhyme at that
That thyme that art say fay fun away.
It came it came it came again
It fell to me to write again to write
And write write be free, for free
Is me that is to see
A picture by tattle.
For time after time
You'll yo yo that I'm fortune of the shore that I'm fanning
along to Dover tomorrow wins
And yet some sunny day
That I have been caught and robbed by hook
And by crook caught and robbed.
You'll soon discover you've gone away. Away in time away
in life.
Yes to a chime and yes to a rhyme
Yes to a chime indeed.
Typically
That fall that winter
That winter's morn a snowy leaf dropped by of gold a special
fall in winter's old stories.

The fall of a leaf skid-le-dee-dee
The fall of a leaf, whizzing
Through the rain until winter came. It came a time when a
little bird's rhyme that was mine
Began my time
To go out to walk and then there was a time when there was a
cataclysmic crash for the rain
Poured down like cymbals and dash.
Get real that means I got soaked. Coasted and toasted and
poached and forlorn.
Song song for you in the toil and the dew that's due that's
certain a song song for you
In the toil and the dew.

Black beauty black beauty
Where for art thou black beauty
Where for thou fence
Thine ladder. By the way
Brown molasses brown molasses to colour the day sun down.
But he who knew black beauty said
What colour art thou fine cow tea the day yea the day the rage
O' the day
Black beauty went away. Someday you'll know that there's a
time and its over
So tears for the time and tears for the mime.

Ex ho-mines librettist a baker's bop and a loaf and by the by.

SONNETS 5

It became a time
A long way off
Where I will blow my horn again
Home again home
Counting the tiles
Again pottery beat.
For sing sang
She sang sing sang song.
You'll soon discovery me
You'll soon sing to my tourney tune.
Sing along fandango
Fandango you me. One day
You'll feel like it writing again.
Writing can be such fun
All over a silver point
World
Where there can be
Where there can be
Flowers a-bloom engines too for a few
More times ago
Times ago soon magic time.
Soon again once again write again
Beat please red again
Write again write again beat yes write.
Yes chip
Chip sir chip chip
Chip wood chip chip chippy.
Carry on calamity train
Calamity, calamity carry on calamity train. One day
You'll know to write it to write it, in
Spontaneity to write it to me.
And soon enough
It became known that life
Is a sad one perchance
You a gone home a sad one

One life. By the way by the way good
Art say. A cheerful
so say-O.

SONNETS 6

And the writing, quoth the man with epicure at the
hairdressers in the noon day.
Stop clowning what happened to something sad without
sadness and what happened say you to
Someone being a clown.
Just for the frill
Of it wearing a gown.
Say I and the ne'er do well.
Sometime in soon I'll offer thee a rhyme.
In soon in time I'll offer thee no rhymes again.

Don't cry for me because I love summer
Time and summer time and some time
Like always I like sing song down a tide O' stone.
Snow on the low bank.
Celebrations, celebration, celebrations for summer's here.

Doesn't seem to be caught again for thee
Prithee pardon pardon a nut. Pardon a nut down town.

Right about around we go
Around around around.

A round a time in space
Me cod a cod of orange
In splendour in splendour be.

Astride a fair fair carousel to sell begone and then it was a
picture of to me time again.

For in the carousel
There was of splendours wonder.

And one time one time more
For art yes art one time iota one time

Fun-dinging ionic.

Funder of time, That time that time more less of mine.

And then one day time it came to me to write some rhymes
some rhyme at that that rhyme that
Art say fay sun away. It came it came it came again it fell to
me to write again to write and write be free, for free is me that
is to see a picture by tattle. For time after time you'll yo yo
that I
Have been caught and robbed by hook and by crook caught
and robbed. You'll soon discover you've gone away. Away in
time away in life. Yes to a chime and yes to a rhyme yes to a
rhyme indeed.
Typically that fall that winter that winter's morn a snowy leaf
dropped by of gold a special fall in winter's old stories.

The fall of a leaf skid-le-dee the fall of a leaf, whizzing
through the rain until winter came.

It came a time when a little bird's rhyme that was not mine
began my time to go out to walk and
Then there was a time.
When there was a cataclysmic crash for the rain poured down
like cymbals.
Get real that means I got soaked. Coasted and toasted and
poached an forlorn. Song song for you
In the toil and the dew that's due that's certain a song song for
you, in the toil and the dew.

Sometimes it's clear I'm clear as can be I'm clear in a kind of
a way I'm as clear as can make it a
Second a do and fin it and wink it and sink it again.
It went for cheer and it went near and for cheer what a
wonderful present to receive on Noel to receive again.

'T was the night before Noel and the fling flung me a bell ring
rung me a bell sing sung me a bell

That I would never past and never before.
Your handwriting is to lyrical and logical too lyrical and
logical get real you know what yes you
Know what a thing.

And that's the end of it all fungal and fungals and Tweedledee
and Tweedledee. So this wheel it spinner much and it spinner
slow puff puff puff. And then one day as it came along
mesmeric and
Magically it came a time the writing went away in a spin and
a short and a day, forever and a way.
Summer and winter and summer in May the top of the fill the
time wrong the time soon gone.
A turn ho for the seasons so. And that's what it does it does a
jig in
The May time.

There was a time before
When all were at work
And all adored and yes all adored and then one day something
happened to you something
Happened to you something happened to you a staff
And a rhyme
A tree and a time
And sadly enough
No building to find
No cockade to announce the meaning of lives
The meaning of lives say
I and the cockade
Would clap and jump
And then one day
He span around and sailed right
Off for he was a bird
And in all wisdom that was
The end of we'll have a nice cup of tea.

And then one day
The music grew faster
Like trains a coming, trains.
And there of course there was a train
A distant sweet a sweet
Old train and in that train
There was a Byrd and by and by
There was a man
This man there was he laughed
A bunch a bunch of bananas
And these are a clown plight samba samba
A do do do writing. And the clown
Had a confession to make as it takes all
Explains all that bobtail
Clown threading his way
'till he believer not and chimer yes.

SONNETS 7

There was a time before when all were at work and all adored and yes all adored and then one day something happened to you something happened to you something happened to you a staff and a rhyme a tree and a time and sadly enough no building to find no cockade to announce the meanings of lives the meanings of lives say I and the cockade would clap and jump and then one day ha span around and sailed right off for he was a bird and in all wisdom that was the end and we'll have a nice cup of tea.

And then one cay the music grew faster like trains a coming, trains. And there of course there was a train a distant sweet a sweet old train and in that train there was a Byre and by and by there was a man this man there was he laughed a bunch a bunch of bananas and these are a clown plight samba samba a do do do writing. And the clown had a confession to make as it takes all explains all that bobtail clown threading his way 'till he believer not and chimer yes.

And now yes and now one upon a time upon a wheel there was a special-er wheel, a wheel so profound that in Latinate talk it ne'er do well that it were to find another such a wheel and this wheel yes, it ponderous much it squeezer.

SONNET 8

It seems one day I went away
Tuna and Scotch egg tuna and Scotch egg and then one day I
went away
With it seems to be sure beef
With a touch of lemon pie
Pie to be sure pie.
By the by it seems to know that one day soon
It caused a delay of the trains a delay
Of the trains and furthermore a delay of the trains.
And then of course there was hero
Cheddar hero cheddar cheerio cheeseboard cheeseboard
cheeseboard
And cheerio. And then of course there was
Of course of course of course of course of course there was of
course of course.
And by the by of course of course
There was heroic cheddar.

Heroic cheddar
Heroic cheddar
There was heroic cheddar.
There was there was there was there was a lovely brick of
cheddar.
And that's the way the cookie crumbles.
Beware beware beware
The unfriendly garden beware.
And then sometime it came too soon
The song song.
And then I must a pinch of salt.